THE DANGER
OF BAD RELIGION

DR. C. RONALD S. WILLIAMS II
PASTOR AND SENIOR ELDER

MOUNT ZION FELLOWSHIP
WWW.MTZIONFELLOWSHIP.ORG

Printed in the United States of America

ISBN: 978-0-9729333-1-5

Preliminary editing by Eric Braun

Substantive editing, proofreading, and design by Joanne Shwed, Backspace Ink (www.BackspaceInk.com)

CONTENTS

Note to Reader 5

Chapter 1: The Fuel of Bigotry 7

Chapter 2: The Danger of Bad Religion 13

Chapter 3: The Colored Side 21

Chapter 4: Is God Still the Judge? 25

Chapter 5: Walking in the Newness of Life.........................31

Chapter 6: Falling Trees 37

Chapter 7: We Can Still Pray 45

Chapter 8: Innocence Is My Guilt.......................................51

Chapter 9: Driven by Faith 55

Note to Reader

IN THIS PAMPHLET, I seek to express my heart and soul. These are just some of my thoughts that I pray will invoke thought in your mind. Have we limited our potential for tolerance and acceptance for others through the medium of bad religion? That is for you to decide for yourselves; however, I thank you for considering what is being offered through this pamphlet. I simply pray that God will be glorified through it.

CHAPTER 1

The Fuel of Bigotry

Bigotry, I fear, has become so tightly intertwined with particular evangelical sects in the United States that bigotry is an unnoticed or unidentified theme of religions in this country. This is not a recent phenomenon, but I have never felt such a broad polarization of the American people as I do today.

ONE DAY, while sitting alongside my grandmother on the front porch of her old clapboard house, she said, "I can smell the rain in the air."

At that time, I did not know rain had an odor, but her many years on this earth had taught her the signs of an incoming storm. After a short while, we heard the rumbling of thunder in the distance and watched the sky darkening from the gathering clouds. My grandmother stood and called all her grandchildren inside of that old house with the long center hallway.

The house would have been considered a shotgun house because the hallway divided the rooms on the east from the rooms on the west. The hallway boasted an old pump organ, a couch, a few chairs, a trunk, and some pictures on the wall.

"Sit quietly and don't move," she told her grandchildren. "When it thunders, the Lord is talking."

She had been taught and truly believed that the Lord was talking in the midst of the thunder and that it was one of the ways of honoring God.

Thunder is powerful and crashing in reverberation. She did not realize that her words and actions perpetuated an unhealthy fear of the Lord and of thunder in our minds and hearts. She was doing the best she knew how to do.

Sunday dinner was always prepared on Saturday evenings because Sunday was the day of rest. These traditions instilled religious beliefs in me that I do not think God intended, but that was what my grandparents believed.

Many people have been taught that anyone whose race or religion was different than their own was a substandard or a superior race of people. It was ingrained in them at an early age.

Bigotry is defined as "intolerance for others who hold a different opinion from oneself." The Apostle Paul wrote in II Corinthians 5:17, "Therefore if anyone is in Christ, he is a new creature; the old things passed away; behold new things have come." I believe this includes changing our thinking and our learned behavior. Could bigotry have been one of the reasons why Paul wrote these words?

What we have learned, which has become a part of our psyche, is often the very thing that damages others and causes separation— even among those of us who call ourselves "evangelicals."

If we are truly evangelicals, shouldn't we be willing to follow God into unchartered territory if it is honoring God? In my opinion, the fear of change is the primary cause of bigotry, hatred, and the lack of progression.

During World War I, a rumor was spread that German-Americans were poisoning food, and President Theodore Roosevelt warned that Germanized socialists were more dangerous than the bubonic plague. The citizens of the United States were warned that Jewish people were plotting to destroy the United States. Somewhere around 1940, a survey found that many Americans considered Jews to be a menace to America because of fear, which motivated many to express bigoted and hateful opinions.

People tend to get angry and form dangerous opinions against things and people that frighten them, and then seek to destroy and keep subservient those whom they do not understand or whose opinions differ from their own.

In more recent times, I have discovered a valuable lesson about fear and trauma and the lasting effects they have on us.

Fear is a strong man; many times, the existence of fear will cause us to rebel against and resist our own success. There is a psychology to fear that can support and fuel bigotry—even racism—that bad religion exploits. If not careful, bad religion can become the malignancy of suffering and apathy. Suffering exists within time and, if allowed, time can bring some level of healing to take place; however, time is not measured by our fluctuating capacity to change and grow, which is why it will always be a tool of those who harm us and those who seek to support and love us.

The fear and trauma that many of us experienced in adolescent years can remain for the rest of our lives. One day, while playing hide and seek with my cousins, I was severely traumatized. Before I could experience any level of healing, I had to go back in my thinking and discover what I had buried deep within my psyche.

Behind my grandparents' home were two barns. To the right was a fig tree, which framed the smokehouse that was located right in front of the tree. I did not know the age of the smokehouse, but it appeared to have been used many times. The smokehouse was the place where my grandfather cured his meats.

My cousin John and I were seeking a place to hide when I heard my cousin Will shout, "Ready or not … here I come!"

I ran to one of the barns to find a spot to hide. As I hid behind the gate of an empty stall, I peeked over the top of the gate in time to see Will run into the other barn where John was hiding and hoped he would find him first, of course. Eventually, both boys walked out of the barn and Will began running toward the barn I was hiding in. I ducked down, stayed as still as possible, and breathed quietly to avoid attention. Will entered the barn and stopped running to carefully analyze all the familiar hiding spots inside. To my surprise, he did not find me.

John was found first, so it was his turn to be the seeker. I was already anticipating hiding somewhere in or around the pig pen.

John centered himself in the yard, closed his eyes, plugged his ears, and began to count, "One ... two ... three ..."

I quickly made my way toward the smokehouse and noticed that the door was open. I entered and, within seconds of analyzing the inside of this place I had never been in before, the door shut behind me. Before I could even think to react, I heard the latch being positioned to secure the door from being opened. I ran to the door to try and open it, but I had been locked inside. Will had locked me in, and I heard him laughing on the outside of the door while I screamed for him to let me out.

Along the back wall of the smokehouse, I noticed a light between two planks. I contemplated trying to kick through and break myself out, but I realized that if I had done that, my grandfather would spank me. I screamed, asking for someone to unlock the door. Finally, the latch on the door was moved, and I was able to escape. I saw my grandmother hanging laundry across the way and ran out to her, grabbing her around the knees and sobbing into her dress. She comforted me and told me to go inside the house, which I did without hesitation.

That experience was the genesis of my fear of being in closed, locked places—even airplanes. After realizing what caused this kind of fear, I have been able to improve because I recognized the genesis of it.

Much of the bigotry, racism, fear, and condescending attitudes we have towards things and people began in our childhood. I believe we need to discover the basis of certain fears and dislikes in order to begin the healing process.

When we allow ourselves to remain products of our environment, we hinder the work of regeneration in our lives and possibly thwart the plan of God for our lives. As we move forward, we hold tightly onto beliefs and practices that we may not even be able to explain. Because these beliefs and practices are so ingrained, it is difficult to comprehend and accept new information that surpasses or counters previous knowledge. In my opinion, our upbringing, our training, the conditions we live in, or a circumstance or belief placed on us for an extended period of time are the metaphorical chains we, as coexisting members of society, have to break.

The counterarguments that challenge our beliefs and opinions do not fuel bigotry; our personal desire to have a tight grip on our beliefs and opinions does. Things from our past have a strong influence on us for the rest of our lives. Among many other things, being locked in the smokehouse is an event I am still struggling with. I never asked Will why he did that to me, and I will never be able to as he has passed away. Forgiveness for him has also been a struggle, but nevertheless it is a choice. Holding onto grudges is too exhausting, and a fist folded tightly disallows the hand to reach out and hold another.

When listening to religious broadcasts, we soon discover stark differences between Pentecostals and Baptists, Catholics and Methodists, and ministries populated with whites and with people of color. Let's go a bit further: There is a difference of belief between Pentecostals and Pentecostals, Methodists and Methodists, and Baptists and Baptists. Evangelicals began to be intolerant of each other because the primary focus and the thing Jesus came to demonstrate and be the example of appears to have been lost: "love."

We are all entitled to our God-given right to have personal beliefs; however, when it restricts us from being neighbors and living in unity with each other, therein lies an issue. Our beliefs, ideologies, and opinions in regard to the secular and the sacred should not intend to impose harm on anyone or turn a blind eye to the opportunities of being a servant of the Lord for our neighbors in their time of need.

Bigotry, I fear, has become so tightly intertwined with particular evangelical sects in the United States that bigotry is an unnoticed or unidentified theme of religions in this country. This is not a recent phenomenon, but I have never felt such a broad polarization of the American people as I do today.

Considering the way we internalize our experiences and receive knowledge during our vulnerable stages, it is not a surprise that we would be defensive when new information challenges them; however, acting with explicit intolerance of other people has been the cause of many lives lost around the world and within our borders.

Even implicit bigotry can be dangerous. Certain messages shared with the American people regarding events and crises in this country have served as a dog whistle for bigots to carry out heinous massacres and other crimes. Racial profiling and discrimination, gender bias, socioeconomic discrimination, and anti-Semitic and other religious aggressions are just a few of the ways in which bigotry shows up in our everyday life. These hateful perpetrators often cannot be reasoned with because what they believe is so strong within them.

Is bigotry a natural tendency of humanity? I don't believe so. I believe it is a mindset that is pushed onto the younger generations as it always has been. After having been programmed to think a certain way, tendencies can ensue—even after becoming consciously aware of them and living intentionally in contradiction of them.

I do not hate my enemies. I do not hate bigots who oppose me. I pray for God's mercy to be upon them and that the Holy Spirit may guide their hearts towards the light of truth. We cannot undo or take back our sins, but an apologetic sinner is more admirable and noble in my eyes than an ignorant and self-righteous one.

CHAPTER 2

The Danger of Bad Religion

I have discovered that radical religion of any nature is destructive, polarizing, divisive, and dangerous. Have we forgotten that religious fervor brought down the World Trade Center? Evangelicals must never forget that thousands have needlessly died because of religious attitudes and fervor. Many were crucified, beheaded, tortured, maimed, and condemned—all in the name of religion.

IF TRUTH IS STRANGER than fiction, then what is a lie? Misdeeds of years past lurk in the depths of unacknowledged pride, arrogance, ignorance, bigotry, and discrimination. If a lie is ungodly, then why do many who claim to be godly embrace the lie of partisanship and religious experience rather than the light of truth?

The power of truth is found in the revealing of God and self. How besetting it is when the past resurrects itself and returns with a fury! Could it be possible that fiction does not just include our hidden wishes, fantasies, and imaginative alternate realities? Could fiction also include our perception of life and how it should be lived, which for many people is sorely based upon personal experiences?

Personal experience becomes dangerous when we make those experiences the law of life for everyone we encounter and when those experiences become the genesis for intolerance, bigotry, hatred, and lack of compassion for anyone whose experiences differ from our own. Do we have to solely be products of personal reality?

I was born in what was known as Lynch County, South Carolina, and partially raised in the small town of Due West. I sat on what was known as the "colored" side of the train station and the doctor's office. I watched the white children swim in the segregated public swimming pool. I drank from the "colored" water fountain and wondered why every man working on the chain gang appeared to be a person of color. Yes, I have picked rows of cotton, which seemed endless, earning only a quarter a day. I attended what was known as the "colored school" and, like many, dealt with unfairness and bigotry. All this was done in the name of religion and the attempt to keep people of color "in their place." Ephesians 6:5 and Colossians 3:22 are just a few of the biblical references that the religious used to justify slavery.

Speaking inadvertently, I would dare say that most of the disunity and problems in our world and country are largely due to religious attitudes and politics. It appears to me that one fuels the other.

I have discovered that radical religion of any nature is destructive, polarizing, divisive, and dangerous. Have we forgotten that religious fervor brought down the World Trade Center? Evangelicals must never forget that thousands have needlessly died because of religious attitudes and fervor. Many were crucified, beheaded, tortured, maimed, and condemned—all in the name of religion.

Faith-based leadership is spiritual if spirituality is understood not as some kind of religious dogma or ideology but rather the domain of awareness where values like truth, goodness, compassion, insight, diversity, and liberty—with the pursuit of justice for all—are free of the biases of political parties and adherence to personalities.

People often fall victim and give glory to what they believe rather than the God they claim to serve. Musicians, for instance, often become intoxicated by their own sweet sounds and are lured to employ lyrics of discrimination, adding to the discord of the symphony of our generation.

One of the many things I have discovered in over forty years of pastoral ministry is that bad religion forces one to look backward, not forward. Many times, people are led to believe that there were once men better and wiser than those who live now. In so doing, we become condescending and intolerant of the living and insist that we shall be governed by the dead. This is not what Jesus came to teach. People must be allowed to live their lives their way, allowing others the right to work out their lives, as long as what we do does not bring harm to another or dishonor God.

It has become glaringly obvious that many people who claim faith in the Lord Jesus Christ are more religious and partisan than they are followers of the teachings and person of Jesus. Many of us claim to love Jesus and embrace Him as our personal savior, but how can we love and embrace someone whom we do not know?

We cannot view or understand the person of Jesus from our Western culture and experience. Many of the attitudes that the religious have turned into issues were not even mentioned by Jesus in the gospels of Matthew, Mark, Luke, or John. He did not come to proclaim intolerance or self-exaltation. He came to be a living example of love and acceptance. He would simply walk away from those who did not embrace or accept his teaching—not condemn them unless they were people who claimed to be of the household of faith.

Jesus was a spokesman for those who did not have social standing. He encouraged people not to be their worst but rather their best selves. Jesus was a voice for the voiceless and a friend to the friendless, even those who were not friends to themselves.

The word "religion" is taken from the Latin root word *religio*, which means "the thing I practice because it is the thing that I believe." The term "evangelical" is taken from the root word *euagge-listes*, which simply means "one who proclaims the gospel."

I have observed that some who claim to be evangelical have taken the term and given it a different definition, only claiming to be evangelical when it aligns with their secular beliefs. Richard Dawkins, a modern British evolutionary biologist and author, is quoted as saying, "Religious fanatics want people to switch off their own minds, ignore evidence, and blindly follow a holy book solely based upon private revelation," or a political party simply because of affiliation.

I do not understand how evangelicals appear to embrace what is going on in our country and not cry out against obvious bigotry, racism, inhumane treatment of immigrants, and the evil disunity that appears to be perpetrated by many who are labeled "evangelical." The United States has always been a beacon of light and hope for a world infiltrated with tyrannical dictators and by people governing people who care more about themselves and their jobs than they do for the people they represent and govern.

We live in a time of shifting culture and moral changes; however, our patriotic and global adherence to what is right must not be extinguished by the stroke of the pen or uninformed resolution of people and partisan organizations that will not take a stand against injustice and unfairness.

A friend of mine told me I was crazy in speaking up against what I consider to be the cause of the downward spiral of our nation. This friend went on to say that Martin Luther King, Jr. would have lived longer if he had kept his mouth shut. It concerned me that this was my friend's thinking. I responded by telling him that if there had not been a voice in the land speaking out against injustice, there would not have been any progression in the effort of minority people to be empowered to fight for equality.

History teaches us that the saviors of this world have been women and men who dared to be different and speak out against the evils of their times while at the same time honoring their God and their faith—not their religious beliefs.

Socrates was poisoned, Aristides ostracized, the Apostle Paul beheaded, Medgar Evers gunned down at his home, Malcolm X murdered, Martin Luther King, Jr. assassinated, and Jesus crucified. Much of the unrest in the Middle East is connected with religious beliefs. We call some of the religious radicals from the Middle East "terrorists"—and some are—but in my experience the terrorists have also included the religious people sitting in church pews most Sunday mornings.

Charles-Louis de Secondat, Baron de La Brède et de Montesquieu (generally referred to as Montesquieu), who was an eighteenth-century French judge, a man of letters, a historian, and a political philosopher, said, "Religious wars are not caused by the fact that there is more than one religion, but the spirit of intolerance."

I believe it is expedient for evangelicals to adopt a mindset of tolerance and acceptance without the semblance of reality television, name-calling, condescending attitudes, or the attempt to humiliate and destroy anyone who has an opinion that differs from theirs. My belief does not mean that we have to agree or give approval to what others may do; it simply means that we should be aware of the hypocrisy that exists in all of us and, once aware, fight against it and seek to walk in the light of truth.

A poet wrote, "Walk in the light, beautiful light. Come where the dew drops of mercy shine bright. Shine all around us by day and by night. Jesus, the light of the world." We must decrease while He increases.

Because of the experiences of bondage and slavery, too many people of color internalize their suffering. This suffering is reinforced by the external experiences while living in a white-dominant society that has historically oppressed nonwhite people and has yet to acknowledge and make an impactful attempt at reconciliation. In fact, this truth—our American reality—is often denied and detested, even to the extent that these ignorant and rejecting attitudes have influenced some community members of color to deny oppressive history, experiences of victims, and the current state of our society.

Denial does not grant liberation of the tortures and misdeeds of yesterday; they should be recognized and admitted, and we should seek to weaken and destroy the power they have held over our lives.

Just as unseen waters can suddenly surge in violent upheaval, so the human heart in unattended pain can finally swell with virulent chaos. We must remember to exhume the buried past and deal with its sorrows and troubles. I believe that many evangelicals choose to bury the misdeeds of yesterday and allow the demons of hatred and bigotry to awaken with new vigor and strength. Governmental and religious leadership can awaken these hidden demons, but we have been given the individual responsibility to make the choice to destroy them or seat them on the thrones of our hearts and thinking.

Adolescent injuries can form an unhealed scab. Hidden infections can form malignancies and poison the entire body if not detected. Scabs fall off of healed injuries; however, if an infection develops under the scabs, it will begin to ooze. Once removed, the infection is revealed. I believe that infections of discrimination, bigotry, racism, and any kind of intolerance are revealed through leadership that has pulled off the cover and allowed the infection to show itself.

Terrorist attacks in America and around the world have substantially increased in the last several years. I believe it is greatly due to the rhetoric of political and religious leaders in our country.

Awareness acknowledged is a necessary requirement for truth to be realized. Religion and politics have the power to bring to the surface that which resides within an individual. Racist and bigoted authority will bring out racism and bigotry in those whom they govern, just as compassionate authority has the potential to encourage others to be compassionate.

Truth is truth. There can be no modification or manipulation of truth; if there is, it is not truth. The light that comes with truth encourages honesty. Honesty is the weakness of those who fear vulnerability or have something to hide. Jesus said He was the truth. Truth does not hide in the crevice of darkness and denial. Where there is an absence of light, truth is abstract at best; however, when the light is allowed to shine, revelation will accompany that light.

II Corinthians 4:1-4 reads, "Therefore, since we have this ministry, as we received mercy, we do not lose heart, but we have renounced the things hidden because of shame, not walking in craftiness or adulterating the word of God, but by the manifestation of truth commending ourselves to every man's conscience in the sight of God. Even if our Gospel is veiled, it is veiled to those who are perishing, in whose case the god of this world has blinded the minds of the unbelieving so that they might not see the light of the Gospel of the glory of Christ, who is the image of God."

Consider this: Is it possible that, in some cases, religion has blinded the religious? Fear is the friend of tyrannical religious authority and the enemy of authority that is righteous. It is paramount that we do not confuse religious mindsets and activity with righteousness.

Where there are bad religious attitudes and mindsets, there will be tyranny. Bad government and religious authority often prey upon the weakness and fear of the religious. The weakness and fear of men make tyranny possible. In my opinion, tyranny is the condition of the heart of the fearful. Tyrants tyrannize only over people who embrace a mindset that fears change and disruption of their beliefs or what they may consider to be a threat to their perceived security.

God is greater than our perceptions concerning Him. In Isaiah 55: 8-9, the prophet writes, with God speaking through him, saying, "For my thoughts are not your thoughts, neither are your ways my ways, declares the Lord. For as the heavens are higher than the earth, so are my ways higher than your thoughts."

We move into turbulent waters when we dare think that we are the final authority. Human behavior is often influenced by things external rather than internal; however, environment, moral history, and religious experience can sometimes prevent sound doctrine and thinking.

Extremism is fueled in environments where tolerance and governmental responsibility or the welfare of all people are neglected.

Radical religion of any nature and tyrannical political dictatorship will create social hopelessness, people who will become apathetic, and others who will become molded by tyranny and not by standards of a just and fair God.

Martin Luther King, Jr. is quoted as saying, "Darkness cannot defeat darkness, only light can do that. Hate cannot defeat hate, only love can do that." I believe we, as evangelicals, must learn to walk in the light of truth and love with the love of Christ.

CHAPTER 3

The Colored Side

There is a definite lack of assimilation of identifying the roots of the massacres and crises of this country, but this polarization always comes back to the proposed solutions. The answer to a problem is contingent on what the problem actually is, and we can never seem to agree on that answer.

FOLLOWING THE READING on public television of a letter I wrote in June 2019, I received many death threats. One man in particular called in to threaten and harass me, stating, "I'm not racist. I just hate N*****s."

I remember growing up in the South, walking down the street, cars driving by, with people on the sidewalks and faces in the store windows. They were all watching, staring.

They would shout at me, "Hey, N*****!"

Someone once said, "Sticks and stones may break my bones, but words will never hurt me." That person was wrong because both hurt. In those moments, I remained strong. I held back tears along with impulsive and emotional retaliation. Sure, words don't show a physical pain but, as I grew up, I always felt there were many things wrong with me. I wanted to love myself, but I didn't really know if I could. The more and more we hear what people say about us—whether or not it is true—the more we begin to question ourselves.

On the phone with the man on public television, aside from my privacy being compromised, his hate did not scare me. Words still hurt, but treatment like that is nothing new to me.

Our collective lives cannot be placed in a box of absolute rights and wrongs because our experiences differ. Oftentimes I have walked away from conversations, wondering why I was not understood or did not understand the perspective of the other person. I soon began to realize that it was because my life experiences had not been the same as theirs.

Our experiences influence our perception of the objective reality. White people cannot understand my experience as a person of color in this country because they cannot live it. Our knowledge is a generalization or stereotypical byproduct of systemic racism with new ways to excuse discrimination. All too often, a man of color is demonized far worse than a white man when they commit the same crime. In fact, a man of color who commits a minor crime is demonized worse than a white man who commits a heinous crime. Selling cigarettes on the sidewalk as a man of color gets him strangled to death on the spot, while raping an unconscious woman in the park at night as a white man will earn him pity because he's got his "whole life" ahead of him. I always noticed that the men of the chain gangs growing up in the South were usually all people of color. What is it about people of color that white racists are so threatened by?

There are several crises going on in this country. Weapons do not select targets; their users select victims, often because of ethnicity. At our borders, we have what seems to be a culmination of modern-day Hooverville towns, which were built by unemployed and destitute people during the Depression of the early 1930s, and the Holocaust, with imprisoned people living in treacherous and inhumane conditions; however, the situation never becomes a mutual topic of discussion because we cannot move past the argument of whether they should have been there in the first place. The well-being of these people cannot wait for us to arrive at an agreement because I feel one may never be met. Emphasis on the "crisis of illegal immigrants" was a dog whistle for white nationalists, with one shooter believing he was delivering "swift and certain justice." In the final analysis between victim and murderer, there are not good people on both sides, especially when the person taking lives is so cold and without remorse.

Whether evangelicals believe that these facilities are inhumane or top-notch, is this Christ-like behavior on our part as Americans? Would Jesus justify something like this?

I believe the acquired immune deficiency of America is the fear of all who believe they are right and everyone else is wrong.

If the only motivation of my approach to life is found in the experience of my past, my progression in life and my intolerance level of others will be greatly challenged. We all have formed opinions that have the potential to divide and polarize the nation. I set myself against political foolishness and the religious mindset of many who claim to be evangelical. I insist that people shall have the right to work out their lives in their own way and allow others that same right—if their individual actions do not negatively infringe on the lives and rights of others.

There is a definite lack of assimilation of identifying the roots of the massacres and crises of this country, but this polarization always comes back to the proposed solutions. The answer to a problem is contingent on what the problem actually is, and we can never seem to agree on that answer.

We come into debate about the experience of people of color in America, for instance. Religion and science have been used historically to justify the enslavement, oppression, and murder of people of color. We know of the Three-fifths Compromise—reached among state delegates during the 1787 US Constitutional Convention due to disputes over how enslaved people would be counted when determining a state's total population—and Jim Crow. There was also a time in this country when immigrants were not eligible to become US citizens if they did not match some of the bogus scientific criteria at the time. Time and time again, nonwhites have been subject to systematic racism legally and illegally.

Jean-Jacques Rousseau—an eighteenth-century Genevan philosopher, writer, and composer—said, "He is great who feeds other minds. He is great who inspires others to think for themselves. He is great who tells you the things you already know, but which you did not know you knew until he told you. He is great who shocks you, irritates you, affronts you, so that you are jostled out of your way and pulled out of your mental rut, lifted out of the mire of the commonplace."

Common ground is simply not an option for some of the issues we face that are rooted in hate and bigotry. The existence of life is one of the many revelations of God; God is within us and, where there is God, there is love. My hope stems from the glory of God. Our capacity to make change must be met with our desire to enact it as well as our humility to recognize the change we need within ourselves.

I cannot sit back and watch the suffering of my fellow creations of God through the subjection of racism. I refuse to learn of another brother's or sister's life taken because of their race. I refuse to stay silent as Muslims and Middle Eastern people are demonized through generalization because of radical extremists.

I believe those who claim to be evangelicals will be held accountable for their fallacious biblical interpretation, their non-Christ-like actions, and their inactions to be Christ-like. In Matthew 28:19-20, Jesus said, "Go ye therefore, and teach all nations, baptizing them in the name of the Father, and of the Son, and of the Holy Ghost, teaching them to observe all things whatsoever I have commanded you: and, lo, I am with you always, even unto the end of the world." We cannot evangelize and antagonize at the same time.

CHAPTER 4

Is God Still the Judge?

*We all know what we like and do not like, accept and
do not accept, all of which gives us the right to make
choices concerning ourselves—not our neighbors.*

MATTHEW 7:1-5 READS, "Do not judge so that you will not
be judged. For in the way you judge, you will be judged; and by
your standard of measure, it will be measured to you. Why do
you look at the speck that is in your brother's eye, but do not
notice the log that is in your own eye? Or how can you say to
your brother, 'Let me take the speck out of your eye,' and behold,
the log is in your own eye? You hypocrite, first take the log out of
your own eye, and then you will see clearly to take the speck out
of your brother's eye."

God is absolute; therefore, He is the ultimate judge. The world
is filled with knowledgeable people and consequentially to religious
dogma and propaganda. We live among people who believe their
opinions to be absolute and truthful. Where do we draw the line
between right and wrong? Is God still the judge of that? As we try

to fit the church into the contextual world, there are many divisions among evangelicals as we identify and propose solutions to various issues.

Jesus came to save us from the fate due to our sinful nature, but while He was with us, He gave us new commandments. He fulfilled the prophesies of the Old Testament and gave us teachings and commandments to live by in the world following His crucifixion and resurrection. Jesus left us with many things and, from those, evangelicals have identified a mission to do God's work in the contextual world. Some of us are heretics, some are bigots, and maybe some of us are doing God's work but just fulfilling the wrong mission.

Luke 6:31-33: "Treat others the same way you want them to treat you. If you love those who love you, what credit is that to you? For even sinners love those who love them. If you do good to those who do good to you, what credit is that to you? For even sinners do the same." Long and arduous are the days that we stray from exemplifying the loving and giving nature that Jesus was among us. "For even sinners love those who love them."

We as evangelicals become consumed with making sure everyone is living life according to our standards, as if it is by our own act that we should be free from sin during our life on this earth. Similarly, in secular regards, we as people—especially in America—become consumed with how people we view as "other" are living in contrast to our customs. In a white, evangelical, heterosexual-dominant culture, those who don't fit in live in outcast. Those who are seen as too different live in this awkward ground between rejection and exile, too severe to be subtle. They exist and reside here; however, their presence is hardly tolerated.

If we love others, that is good, as Jesus tells us in the scripture above. If we love others as God loves us, then others will know God's love. If they love us in return, then they also love God. We overquestion those who demonstrate love and whether or not they are saved. Relationship with God is personal. What good comes from a man of faith who does harm to others falsely in accordance with God's will when he judges another who only loves others but is not explicit about his faith in the divine?

It is not my intention to imply that there are times when we earn exemption from canon law because we do not; however, it is not within our own capacity to break from sin in our lifetime. That day will come when we stand before God and He gives us new life!

James 4:11-12 reads, "Do not speak against one another, brethren. He who speaks against a brother or judges his brother, speaks against the law and judges the law; but if you judge the law, you are not a doer of the law but a judge of it. There is only one Lawgiver and Judge, the One who is able to save and to destroy; but who are you to judge your neighbor?"

Since the days of antiquity, men and women have exploited and tried to possess that which belongs to God, and God alone. One of those dynamics is judging. The scripture gives me the right to judge one person, and that person is myself. 1 Corinthians 11:31, "... if we judged ourselves rightly, we would not be judged."

The judgment of mankind is a flawed and imperfect judgment. Evangelicals, have we gotten it twisted? Generally speaking, none of us has a complete and perfect handle on what is right or wrong. We must not infringe upon the religious, legal, political, or social rights of another. However, integrity teaches us to operate under the laws and bylaws of the local assembly, community, city, state, and country. If a person desires to become a citizen of a particular country or a member of an organization, one abides by the rules of that organization. However, one cannot force others outside that organization to abide by cultural standards. Sometimes there is a dress code or dues to pay within the organization, but I cannot expect anyone to abide by my standard outside of that group of people.

We all know what we like and do not like, accept and do not accept, all of which gives us the right to make choices concerning ourselves—not our neighbors. In the scriptures, I have not found a place where Jesus condemned people for their lot in life. However, I have read where He helped a woman who had been caught in adultery, gave sight to the blind, fed the hungry, and encouraged a beg-gar—all without seeking anything in return or expecting that they become living epistles and examples of what He had done for them, and only if they chose to do so.

As the world continues to become more globalized and con-sumed in capitalism, this selflessness that Jesus showed is contrary to the attitudes expressed in our society today. We are hesitant and resistant to giving if there is nothing guaranteed for us in return. As a consequence, many suffer in this country and worldwide because we do not extend a hand to give if it does not receive or if it leaves the individual vulnerable and without defense. We as a society and in our various organizations—political, religious, and even charitable—are too selfish and timid to do what is necessary to serve people.

I believe the emotion that fuels one's need to be in control and condemn others is fear, which the scripture declares that God has not given us. If the only strength in my life is found in the experi-ences of my past, my progression and tolerance level will be greatly challenged. All of us have formed opinions that have the potential to divide us. Our opinions of each other should not be founded upon race, creed, religion, politics, or past experience.

So many people are experiencing a slow, silent, emotionally pain-ful death because of their fear of judgment and rejection. Much of this has been caused by the judgmental attitudes of others around them. Rather than being their true selves in Christ, they hinder their lives and potential for fear of what others will say or think of them. Sometimes it is in adolescence that we learn to please everyone except God and ourselves.

I believe that personal judgment is one of the factors contribut-ing to the demise of the local assembly and our country. A woman who became one of the most popular spiritual and gospel vocalists of the 1950s and '60s was Mahalia Jackson. Her soulful singing was considered ungodly and carnal when she first began her ministry. Many churches would not have her come to minister because they were not accustomed to her style of singing. They thought her singing belonged in a bar or nightclub. However, she pressed through to become one of the most called-on gospel singers in the country. If she had succumbed to the opinions of others, she would have disappeared into the dark alley of failure and defeat, but she pressed her way and succeeded in what she believed God had called her to do—regardless of the opinions and judgments of others in the church.

I too have experienced something very similar. I had directed and played the keyboards in the church where my father was the pastor for a few years before heading off to college. On campus was an existing gospel choir, and the president of this choir asked me to direct it. I did everything in my power to elevate the ministry of this choir and bring in other musicians and instruments, but I was told that I could not bring in drums or horns—and not even an organ—because they believed those instruments were of the devil.

One may never stop learning how to distinguish between religious fervor and righteousness. Throughout scripture, we read where God had to call people out of their comfort zones in order to receive glory in their lives. Tradition and religious beliefs can be offensive when forced upon others. I suggest that we—the evangelicals of the United States—need to step out of our comfort zones. We believe others are holding themselves back from receiving God's glory; however, we are not only the perpetrators of our very accusation, but we are also holding ourselves back.

By the action, and inaction, of governing and capable powers in this country, people suffer from a lack of equity to be free from poverty, discrimination, and endangerment. Through dogmatic ignorance, victims are shamed and villainized in their own suffering while perpetrators receive mercy and sympathy. We have blurred the line between right and wrong. By scrambling and twisting definitions, whose will are we carrying out? Certainly not God's!

Religion guides us on what to believe, how to act on our beliefs, and how to interpret the world around us. Spirituality is the experience of divine revelation through all that is observable and sensible. The church is supposed to be where believers of Christ Jesus can join together in community to grow and strengthen faith and worship the Lord. For centuries, the church has developed rituals and canon law and attempted to form assimilation of people by beliefs. The church's use of religion has too often failed to continue to be contextual in discipleship and mission. Religion in many cases has become a tool for propaganda.

The Bible is holistic in its message, and yet the Christian community is fragmented, especially due to varying degrees of interpretation of scripture. Some denominations have built reputations on how they shame persons into a life of structure, consisting of little individualized experience. Without experience, we may only have faith by reason, which by our own capacity can be problematic. Spirituality is supplemental and essential for religion. Although life may be a group experience, it is all too often forgotten how personal life is, similar to our relationship with God.

The distinction of right and wrong has become too subjective. As I call out those of higher platforms who twist truths and make implausible judgments, I'm sure that eyes reading this would accuse me of the same. If their "right" and "wrong" is not true, then who am I to say that mine is? Individuals are not all good or all bad, but explicitly we can observe and identify which one they lean toward. It all comes down to what we know and what we intend to do with it. We are here to take care of each other, but what purpose are we fulfilling when our perception of "good" is carried out at the expense of loving, gentle, and good fellow creations of God?

CHAPTER 5

Walking in the Newness of Life

*How can we as people in the United States move towards
newness of life as a nation? There are many things in this
country's history that may forever stain our attitudes on
different matters. Rightfully so, we cannot forget about these
things. Forgiveness will come for those when it is earned,
but we must always remember the downfalls of our nation's
history so that we can ensure they are not repeated.*

A BIBLICAL PENTECOSTAL experience is where one begins to walk in the newness of life. For some, the experience is instantaneous; for me, the beckoning call to a new and fresh life was prolonged. It all began in Due West, South Carolina. I grew up going to church because I had to, not primarily because I wanted to.

One hot Sunday morning in church, the choir sang a hymn called, "Come Thou Almighty King," which touched something deep within me. I felt a strange, burning feeling moving inside. After church, we went home, and I sat down at the old upright piano in our family's living room. I had never had a lesson and never practiced on my own. There was something about that song—the chords, the notes, the sound of the keys, and the choir singing together triumphantly—that I just could not get over. I began pressing keys here and there, listening to the hymn in my head. Single keys graduated to chords and a bass line. Before I knew it, I was playing "Come Thou Almighty King," and my family gathered all around to sing and celebrate.

Poppa (my grandfather) was a bass singer second to none. I'll never forget Poppa's voice as he came through the hallway singing.

When he saw that it was me playing, he cheered loudly, "Good God Almighty! I told you that boy was different! He's something else."

After that day, I would walk through the pinewoods, humming the hymns I heard from church. I think it was the beauty of the pinewoods and the music at church that guided me to seeing the beauty in other things of God's creations.

Several years later, I had my real Pentecostal awakening experience. During my senior year of undergrad, our choir made a guest performance at my father's church in Chicago. My father introduced the choir, but what came after was a bit of a surprise. My father began humming. It was a vague tune that I could not follow on the organ. The humming effused into moaning as the congregation joined in. The humming evolved to words, and a mysterious charisma evoked among the crowd. He began to sing, "A charge to keep I have, a God to glorify. A never dying soul to save and fit it to the sky." The charged atmosphere brought tears to everyone's eyes, as they did mine. It was not like any church service I had ever experienced up to that point.

When we got back to school, I immediately went to my dorm and sat at my desk. I wasn't a student of the Bible; I was only familiar with a few psalms, which was shocking being a preacher's kid, I'm sure. However, I opened up my Bible and the book fell to the prophecy of Isaiah, chapter 26. The third verse leaped out at me: "I will keep you in perfect peace if your mind is stayed on me." I didn't know what to make of it.

Months later, I graduated and was back in Cleveland in the attic of my family's house. I went from strutting proudly in my black graduation robe across campus to being depressed back home. I didn't find work for the first three weeks. An old friend invited me to a revival service. I accepted and picked her up that Saturday. I hadn't been to church the whole time I'd been home.

The preacher that evening was a young man from California—short but with a voice strong and full of authority. My heart was ignited by his compelling command from the Gospel of John: "You must be born again!" Through his vigor of the word, I surrendered. Something awakened in me that evening. Inexplicable things can only be understood in time through experience and revelation, and my revelation hit me that night. After that, I answered the call to a relationship with God as well as the call to ministry.

Out of all the thoughts I have written in these chapters, this one is mostly testimonial. To come into a newness of life is only through a Pentecostal experience. Relationship with God is a shared experience, but it is primarily a personal one, and the means by which we are touched and moved by the Holy Spirit is individualized. God reached out to me in the way I needed to hear that call. I believe God has sent different kinds of people to spread the Word in specialized ways—whether it be social class, race, culture, or language—as he did in Acts 2. God is accepting of His people, even if we are not all the same.

One who walks in the newness of life does not live righteously by self-exaltation. The people who initially experienced Pentecost were from different walks of life. The disciples, for instance, were tax collectors and fishermen, and were not active members of the church, probably with the exception of Thomas. The majority were gentiles. Peter and a few others were Jewish, but they were not religious Jews. The disciples praised God and, as we are told, were favored by all people. The reason I believe they were so liked was because they were freshly saved and had not formed their own personal opinions and doctrines. They were a refresh to tradition. The rest of the city did not shun or try to avoid them but instead joined them because of the godly example those who experienced Pentecost set.

There was no problem until the established religious organizations and mindsets came to attack them because of their own practices and politics, which influenced what they believed. That's what we have today with evangelicals. Could that be why we have so many denominations? We formed our own practices; however, just because we believe something doesn't make it right.

Consider the story of a girl who loved her mom's ham. The girl noticed that her mother always cut off the front and the back.

When asked by her daughter why she did this, her mother replied, "That's the way my mother did it."

The girl then asked her grandmother the same question and received the same reply: "That's the way my mother did it."

The girl's great-grandmother was still alive to answer the same question and replied, "Because I didn't have a pot big enough to fit the ham."

We all fall into bigotry because, most of the time, that's all we know unless we have had a Damascus road experience as the apostle Paul did when he saw Jesus. The focus there is not that he was physically blinded; it was that he was thrown into a conundrum. Everything he thought he knew wasn't true. One of the greatest persecutors of the church had to turn around and apologize. Isaiah 6: "In the year King Uzziah died, that's when I saw the Lord." He was the pastor for the king and the prophet of the land, but the grandeur, power, success, and greatness of Uzziah blinded Isaiah to the greatness of the Lord. When he saw Him, he said, "I've been wrong all these years. I'm an unclean man living among unclean people. I heard the great commission. Whom shall we send? Who will go for us? Here am I Lord, send me!"

How can we as people in the United States move towards newness of life as a nation? There are many things in this country's history that may forever stain our attitudes on different matters. Rightfully so, we cannot forget about these things. Forgiveness will come for those when it is earned, but we must always remember the downfalls of our nation's history so that we can ensure they are not repeated.

I believe we are already witnessing the travesty of the past as themes of past sins of this country reappear in our modern context. They say things get worse before they get better. I heard someone say recently that they believe racism is dying and, like a vicious animal, it surges in defense for one last attack in an attempt to escape its death. I think such a statement dwells in oblivion and modesty. People debate about whether racism is worse now than it was a few years ago, and perhaps it is subjective, but I know my own experience with it. One thing no one can ever claim is that racism ever died. Racism never went away.

What I see as a newness of life for the United States is perhaps too ideal a thought to ponder. I see people of color living without being hated or killed for existing. We do not cut funding for public education. Appropriate actions are taken for gun violence and drug epidemics. People of the LGBTQ community are not discriminated against or outcast and do not live in fear for their own survival. Higher education is at least affordable. We take care of our elderly and our veterans. I dream of leaders who do the right thing and make selfless sacrifices to bring about change for the benefit of all people in this country. I hope one day that America does not ignore or justify the sins of its past and present but rather acknowledges them and always seeks ways to be a land of united people, as we should be.

CHAPTER 6

Falling Trees

May we love our neighbors as ourselves? If God is love and God is the one who connects us all, then love is the way in which we must demonstrate our connection with one another. Too many have allowed hate into their hearts.

AS I PROPOSED in the previous chapter in reference to Acts 2, for us to come together as a people begins with a Pentecostal experience. The scripture says, "all those who had believed were together and had all things in common." Obviously, they did not literally have all things in common, but the things they did have in common were so major that their differences could not influence them to be pulled apart. They had one mind; they were sharing their possessions with one another and with others in need and were favored by those around them. The rest of the gentile community did not shun them but rather desired to join them because of the godly example they set. If we are to be evangelicals, there must be some kind of common denominator, which I believe is Jesus.

Some years ago, two of my assistants were not getting along; I could just tell. I invited them both to my home one day to try and mediate the relationship. I have a lighthouse at one of the ends of the house that overlooks the woods. At the top of the lighthouse, I told them to gaze over everything below and in the distance.

"What do you see?" I asked.

They both replied, "We see trees."

Much to their amusement, I said, "Good. Give me some characteristics."

"They all have branches," they answered, standing quietly while still looking at the forest.

"They're all bare because winter has set in," I offered.

They continued to scan the trees as I spoke.

"All the branches are crooked and knotted," I continued. "Somehow, they find their way to go up. They all go in their own direction. All the branches, as different as they may be, are still connected to the trunk. They all live and grow because of the trunk. That's their common denominator." I paused for a moment as I began to delight in the view too. "When spring comes, they sprout leaves and flowers. You won't be able to see what's happening underneath because the leaves provide the shade and covering for the limbs. Then, when the limbs become bare again, they will still be connected to the trunk. It's alright to be different, as long as you maintain the connection."

During the 1980s, I remember one popular saying: "Have faith in yourself." I believe that was a message many needed to hear then, and there are still those who need to have more faith in themselves now. Believing in ourselves empowers us to grow in our individualities and to divert from unnecessary tradition, but there are too many who have developed too much faith in themselves and even in the evangelical community. It almost becomes questionable as to who they have more faith in: themselves or the living God?

Like branches, we grow in different directions. We produce and invent as God has gifted us as co-creators, but we must remember who the glory belongs to. We must remember the One who connects us all: the One Triune God!

I think one of the ways in which we differentiate ourselves from those around us are the things that we obtain either externally or internally. The branches of a tree grow leaves, and some produce beautiful flowers and fruit in the spring. When the winter comes, the branches are stripped bare. They are vulnerable. They are not very different from the others. They are nothing without the trunk. No matter the season, their connection to the trunk holds them together. Jesus said in the gospel of John 15:5, "I am the vine, ye are the branches; he that abideth in me, and I in him, the same beareth much fruit: for apart from me ye can do nothing."

I wish there was no partisanship or denominations. I wish we just devoted our conscience and served God. Then arises the question, "How do I serve God?" 1 John 4:7 reads, "Beloved, let us love one another, for love is from God, and whoever loves has been born of God and knows God."

May we love our neighbors as ourselves? If God is love and God is the one who connects us all, then love is the way in which we must demonstrate our connection with one another. Too many have allowed hate into their hearts. Psalms 51 says, "Create in me a new heart oh God," but, if the heart is not willing to change, it declines the invitation of a Pentecostal experience and cannot experience the togetherness that a changed heart would. If we are harboring hate towards those who are different due to race, gender, socioeconomic status, nationality, and religion, then we are most likely carrying old traditions and beliefs. The solution is for our hearts to be made new by God.

Many of us have become somewhat knowledgeable of the effect trees have on our ecosystem and the role trees play in our environment. In a forest, there are many varieties of trees and plants. A maple tree may be growing next to an oak tree, and the oak right next to an evergreen of some sort. The hickory, walnut, birch, apple, cherry, and many other genres of trees all exist and thrive together in the same wood.

A few decades ago, I learned a valuable lesson about forests and trees. Our local assembly had purchased ten acres of wooded land in order to erect our new worship facility and cleared enough land for the future expansion and parking lot. We cleared approximately five of the acres and sold the timber. It was a fascinating experience in that some very large trees were cleared, which indicated that the land was sturdy and could support the weight and size of the new facility. The project engineer had boring holes drilled to see the depth of the bedrock in order to provide support for the building, and the boring hole report was good. We were ready to go forth and build. However, as soon as the backhoe began to dig, we ran into water and discovered that we were building right over an underground river. This was surprising in that the contractors hit water at only about three feet down. How could this be? We then understood that this kind of situation normally could not support the growth of the size of these hardwood trees without them falling over.

At this point, my first revelation about trees was realized. An arborist was called in to assess the issue.

"How could this be?" I asked him.

He responded by saying that the trees supported and held up each other, and that is how they were able to reach that size in this type of soil. "The underground water kept the trees hydrated, and the nutrients in the soil produced trees of this size."

Each tree—regardless of the type of tree it may have been—supported the other trees around it. Some of the trees produced apples, some walnuts, some cherries, and some sap, but they were all growing together in nature's harmony, providing shelter for birds and animals as well as a beautiful landscape.

I believe Jesus taught that we who are believers and followers of Him should be like the trees in the forest. We may come from different backgrounds and experiences and have different gifts, but we can be supportive of one another and hold each other up. The trees collectively form something of a structure. The inside of the forest feels calmer than outside. Together, the trees block rain and wind and protect each other; they thrive together. When a tree falls, it is loud; it shakes the ground; it is dramatic. If one tree dies, the trees it helped support and were supported by it begin to die also, and other trees surrounded by them begin to die too. A community of trees that once all stood becomes a desolate tree cemetery.

In this metaphor, we are the trees, and we are also the cutters. I have found that some of the meanest people sit in church pews every Sunday and will not support or befriend anyone who has an opinion that differs from their own. Some of these people even spitefully tear down others and justify themselves in the process. We cannot continue to tear each other down. When limbs and branches are amputated, a tree may continue to stand, but it's never as full as it once was. The solution to our problems cannot be sought through the primary instinct of removal. As evangelicals, we must support others. Weak trees, trees of a different variety, and even big trees—as strong as they may seem—all need each other.

There is power in connection and thus destruction in the lack thereof. The message is clear. To the evangelicals, let our connection to God through Christ Jesus be our connection with other people; however, do not let it be a standard that we use to build borders between us and other people. Follow Christ and let our connection with him lead us to fellowship with other evangelicals, but also let our connection with our Creator lead us to our connection with all of God's creations! Nothing can diminish the fact that we are all fearfully and wonderfully made in God's image. Our connection is always there, and it is up to us to acknowledge it and act on it. Do not hide insecurities behind false pride any longer. May we come together in mutual connection and form a garden of beautiful trees, for we are all God's children!

On the remaining acres of our property, valuable trees were thriving. The board made the decision to sell some of the trees in that section. A few years later, I began to notice the trees that had surrounded the timbered ones began to die. I soon discovered that, when a forest is partially timbered and stumped, it will sometimes damage the root system of surrounding trees. Once this occurs, the root system of surrounding trees cannot recover. Those damaged trees begin to die a slow death and become vulnerable to disease and insect infestation. When we, as evangelicals, tear each other down, we are exposing ourselves to a slow death. No one is one hundred percent correct all the time. We cannot afford to be "so heavenly minded, until we become no earthly good."

I believe it is imperative for those of us who stand on the rock of the gospel to realize that we are not the answer; Jesus is. We must not be guided by religious affiliation or political partisanship but rather by love, peace, and of course His Holy Spirit.

God has reserved judgment for Himself. Being in Christ prepares believers for heaven. Christ in believers prepares them for life on Earth. Believers represent Him on Earth as He represents believers in heaven. Jesus is the Son of God, who came to Earth to tell us about God, and He is the Son of man, who went back to heaven to shield us from the wrath of God.

Believers in Christ can face the Father; Christ in believers can defeat the enemy. Yes, the enemy of bigotry, hatred, jealousy, fear, judgmental attitudes, and every other negative force can be defeated. "He ever liveth to make intercession for His people" (Hebrews 7:25). What could be accomplished for the kingdom of God if the church supported each other the way the trees do in the forest?

God, Himself, sets the course for our lives; however, many times we are blown off course by our own experiences, wills, and desires.

As the story goes, three trees grew on a hill by the side of the sea. One day, the three trees had a conversation concerning what they wanted to become once they reached maturity.

The first tree said, "When I grow up, I want to be used in building a great palace in order that all royalty may walk by and admire my fine grains and rich color."

The second tree said, "I want to be used in building a great ship of war in order that the strength of my wood can be appreciated."

The third tree said, "I want to be used in building a pulpit in a great temple from which people's lives will be changed."

Before long, the woodcutters came to the grove. One by one, the trees felt the blow of the ax.

The first tree was taken to be used in a building, but the building was not a palace; it was a stable. In this stable, the savior of the world was born.

The second tree was taken to be used in the building of a sea vessel, but the sea vessel was not a mighty ship of war; it was a fishing vessel. In this boat, Jesus preached to thousands.

The third tree was taken to be used in the making of the greatest pulpit the world had ever known; it was the cross on which they hung the savior of the world.

Evangelicals: We must get back to the place of accepting the will of God and accepting the differences of others.

CHAPTER 7

We Can Still Pray

Jesus came for damaged people, but we are not going to get help until we recognize that we are the one who's jacked up. We've been through twenty, thirty, forty, fifty, sixty, or seventy years of being damaged, and each formed a layer. Over time, tough and beaten skin begins to callous. Why does change bring on such discomfort? Why is it much easier to revert to the messed-up ways we had before? Our issues, egos, and bad habits have thick skin.

IN THINKING ABOUT the power of prayer and how we pray, I am reminded of the story about King Saul. In 1 Samuel 10, in one chapter, we find the prophet of God—Samuel—talking to a man named Saul. In the first chapter, Samuel prophesied over him, which is a form of prayer. Then he anointed him, which is another form of prayer. God told Samuel that He was going to change his heart. Within one chapter, everything that God told Samuel would happen to Saul happened. God changed Saul's heart but, within the same chapter, when they came to get Saul, he had gone back to the Aramaic word *khalid*, which means "his own issues." The townspeople had to get him when the prophet was calling for him and bring him out for him to do what God said to do.

This story tells me that God can change a person's heart, but it's up to the person to change their mind. Be ye, Paul said, transformed by the renewing of your mind (Romans 12:2). All the prayer that Samuel the prophet had done for Saul amounted to nothing because Saul did not want to acknowledge his own issues. I've been praying for some people for a long time, hoping they would change. What the Lord has shown me is that some people will never change.

The rich, young ruler came to Jesus and said, "What must I do to inherit eternal life?"

Jesus said, "Go sell all that we have and give it to the poor" (Luke 18:18-23).

The ruler simply walked away We don't read anything about Jesus praying for him. That is where the church gets messed up: parents praying for children who don't want to change, children praying for parents who don't want to change, and friends praying for friends who don't want to change. Our prayers will not amount to anything when we are dealing with a person who does not want to acknowledge that something's wrong with them. What the Lord told me, I do believe, was to stop praying for them and start praying for ourselves to give us the wisdom to know how to deal with this person. In other words, we must realize and accept when to walk away.

Some individuals in our lives, it seems, were deliberately placed to keep us messed up. They keep us on the edge of our seat. We've done all that we know how to do to help them, but, at some point, they revert back to the kind of person they shouldn't be. They want the gain, but they can't accept the necessary loss.

When I look at Saul, and how the man of God for the hour—Samuel—had prayed for Saul, prophesied for Saul, and anointed Saul, Saul continued to go back to his own way and to his own baggage. It was not Samuel's baggage. That's where we mess up. We try to carry somebody else's baggage. We've done everything we could to help some people with their baggage; soon, as they get their butt on their shoulders, they go right back to where they were. The disciples had just come through a storm with Jesus. Jesus sent them to the other side. They had to go through a storm to get to the other side. When there's something that God wants us to see or something that God wants us to do, many times storms will arise to prevent us or try to stop us from going to the other side.

As we continue reading the scripture, and because we are so drama-oriented, we sensationalize the scripture. Jesus went to Gadara and met a man, who was messed up, in the cemetery, just as Saul was messed up when Samuel had met him. The scripture says, in 1 Samuel 10, that God changed his heart. There are people in every local assembly where God may have changed their hearts, but they did not allow their hearts to change their minds. The scripture says that this man was dwelling among the tombs, and no one was able to reason with him. He was locked up as was Saul, in his own stuff.

The mind is a powerful thing because this man was dwelling among dead things. There are people in our lives who just cannot stop dwelling with dead things. A better translation would be that things brought them distress, depression, and anger towards everybody except themselves. People who dwell among dead things always project just like Saul. Every time something happened, Saul always redirected blame. Everything the prophet told him when he did not obey had an adverse effect. He was not enlightened. He was resentful of everyone else.

Here is the perplexing part of this narrative: As oppressed and possessed as he was, the spirits, demons, or issues that controlled him recognized Jesus! They shouted on Sunday morning. They danced on Sunday morning. They waved their hands in the service. Demons recognize their Creator, but this man had layers of demonic activity and damage. Each layer was fortifying the previous layer. This man was extremely damaged, and that's why nobody could talk to him. Some of us think that, because we grew up in church, we're not damaged. Every last one of us has a level of damage. If we were not damaged, then why did Jesus come? Jesus came to help us get over the effects of our damage.

Jesus came for damaged people, but we are not going to get help until we recognize that we are the one who's jacked up. We've been through twenty, thirty, forty, fifty, sixty, or seventy years of being damaged, and each formed a layer. Over time, tough and beaten skin begins to callous. Why does change bring on such discomfort? Why is it much easier to revert to the messed-up ways we had before? Our issues, egos, and bad habits have thick skin.

Jesus came to that damaged man who had been living amongst doubt, lies, depression, distress, anger, anxiety, and worry; that man who had been damaged by many people for years. The demons (damage) that controlled the man spoke to Jesus, not the man.

The damaged man looked up and said to Jesus, "Oh Jesus, what do I have to do with You?"

We ignore our damage, which is the source of our shame. It seems simpler to blame somebody else because, if we don't, that means we have to deal with ourselves. When I seek God with my whole heart, when God places His purpose and His plan upon my life, and when I embrace His purpose and His plan for my life, God gives me the desire of my heart because my heart is lined up with His heart. At this point, I can truly say that I trust God to fulfill the plan that He has placed upon me. "As Jesus said, nevertheless, not my will but Thine be done" (Luke 22:42).

I can hope and pray all I want, but until what I'm hoping and praying for lines up with the will of God—especially if God has a call on my life and especially if God has something He wants me to do—it will not. So many things in my life have fallen through the cracks and failed because it was my desire and not God's desire.

All over this country, many people have been wondering what is going on and saying, "Lord, I thought I had it right!"

We may have had it right, and we may have it right, but when we ponder our perception of the activity in the world, let us not forget to evaluate the role we have in it and our contributions to it. What is our current effect, and what would we like our effect to be? How can we exercise prayer? We can start by praying for ourselves. There is always room to grow, and there is always love to give.

There was a time in my life, shortly after entering the ministry of the preached word of God, that I really thought I knew what I was talking about. When I go back to some of the teachings, the truth is that I feel stupid. The scripture becomes so real to me when God said, "My thoughts are not your thoughts; and My ways are higher than your ways" (Isaiah 55:8).

When I look at scripture—from Genesis through Revelation—I see those who had visions, as Abraham did, but they could not make out every dynamic or every aspect of what was going on because that is the way of God. When God gives a vision, faith must be employed on our part. I don't know exactly what I'm seeing, but I know I'm seeing something. When something has been hard-wired into our thinking, our heart will not change until we recognize that something is wrong with us.

Prayer is demonstrated in many forms. Popularly in our common use, it is a conversation. More often than not, it is a request to God to uphold or deliver something in such a way or plan that we have already plotted out: "God, please help so-and-so change to this, so that this thing can happen, and let it happen this way."

Neighbor, prayer happens, but the power is with God and the change is in our willingness. Let's pray in every way we know how, but let us not be discouraged. Let's hold onto our faith.

The Lord is not finished.

CHAPTER 8

Innocence Is My Guilt

We may differ religiously and be affiliated with different political
parties; however, we can agree on fairness, equality, liberty, and
justice for all. We can agree that all men were created equal and,
in this nation, all Americans have certain inalienable rights.

INHERIT THE WIND was an American film drama released
in 1960, inspired by the famous Scopes Trial of 1925, in which
a high school teacher was arrested and prosecuted for teaching Charles Darwin's theory of evolution. In the movie, the
townspeople were all extremely religious and what they called
"evangelical."

Once the high school teacher was arrested and placed in jail, the
townspeople marched around with burning crosses as they chanted,
"Death to the teacher!"

They marched around with their evangelical religious fervor,
which almost caused the lynching of this teacher. They were guilty of
insurrection, but the root of their guilt was due to a sense of innocence they had. They were doing what they had been taught to do

and believing what they had been taught to believe because of their experience and the teaching of their parents and authority figures in their day. Such a vicious act cannot be justified or excused, but, when considering the root of an issue, their innocence is that they acted on what they believed, or rather asserted, to be the truth.

That day has not changed.

Cicely Tyson is quoted as saying, "Many times, the guilt of supremacists, bigots, and white nationalists is found in their innocence."

I also believe those words; however, I do not understand how anyone who has an adherence to the Lord Jesus Christ can afford to stay in the place of the kind of supremacy and hatred simply because someone has a different skin color or religious affiliation. Jesus said, "if any man be in Christ Jesus, he is a new creature, old things pass away and behold, all things are new" (II Corinthians 5:17).

In my studies, all the religions I have come across devise codes covering their conduct. Although their traditions may be different today, in the old days, the maidens in the Hopi Tribe dressed their hair in one way and the married women in another. If a married woman clothed herself like a maiden, she was regarded as past redemption and would be killed. In Christian history, one of the Ten Commandments that is against making graven images was founded on the fallacy that sculpture and idolatry were one in the same. The Puritans believed that the arts of sculpture and painting were both idolatrous and that instrumental music was the work of the devil. While a few believed that instruments like the organ were proper and right, stringed instruments were thought of as harmful and tended to lascivious pleasing.

Anne Hutchinson, a seventeenth-century Puritan spiritual advisor and religious reformer, cut the Gordian Knot of law at a stroke of the pen by saying, "Get the grace of God in your hearts." At that point, things will change.

When Jesus plucked the ears of corn on the Sabbath Day, He violated Jewish law and showed them then and at various other instances that He had little regard for the laws governing conduct.

He did not see them as divine and in part came to show how laws can change and are not timeless in relevance. More often than not, people who have taken such a view have been regarded as anarchistic and considered enemies of the state. Consequently, they were considered to be dangerous people to be silenced.

In Elbert Hubbard's book, *Little Journeys to the Homes of American Statesmen*, it is written that, "During the Civil War, it was assumed by a large contingent that if we believed in equal rights for the colored man we were desirous of having your daughter marry a 'n*****.'"

A similar theme is laid for other groups facing oppression: "Many good men assume that if you believe in giving the right of suffrage to women, you want your wife to run for the office of constable. There are those who assume that men who do not go to church play cards; those who play cards chew tobacco; those who drink whiskey beat their wives; therefore, all men should go to church. All of Anne Hutchinson's trouble came from inferences. These inferences were the work of the clergy."

In my opinion, not much has changed as it relates to the beliefs of those who consider themselves to be religious and even evangelical. Some may disagree in their perception of the times. What danger is there in equal rights? What about in women holding clergy positions and other types of leadership? If we can agree that all people are equally deserving, we may find ourselves silently advocating for such matters; however, when the rights and well-being of deserving equal creations of God are being violated, advocacy can no longer be silent and reserved.

I truly believe that people who have spent the majority of their lives believing a thing will retain that thing in their minds and believe it until something happens to change that mindset. Scripture speaks of strongholds and fortifications that can take hold of our minds. Could that be the reason why the Apostle Paul spoke in Romans chapter 12: 1-2, "… therefore, I urge you brother and by the mercies of God, to present your bodies a living and holy sacrifice, acceptable to God, which is your spiritual service of worship. And do not be conformed to this world, but be transformed by the renewing of your mind, so that you may prove what the will of God he is, that which is good and acceptable and perfect."

We may never be "one nation under God, with liberty and justice for all" as long as we allow our religious and political beliefs to divide us and become the basis of hate and intolerance. In the prophecy of Amos 3:3, we are given to know that men cannot walk together unless they walk in agreement.

We may differ religiously and be affiliated with different political parties; however, we can agree on fairness, equality, liberty, and justice for all. We can agree that all men were created equal and, in this nation, all Americans have certain inalienable rights.

CHAPTER 9

Driven by Faith

Very few people are comfortable with themselves. They
long for something to make themselves feel good, and
church is a place where people may go to get that.
Evangelicals, however, use religion in a toxic way.

HAD I NOT grown up in the church, been the son of a
preacher, or had my own spiritual experience, I would not have
taken the call to ministry or had any desire to be involved with
the Christian religion. This is certain. The things I see of the
Christian community—the judgment, the arrogance, and all
the other behaviors that Jesus did not focus on—are the things
to which many contemporary evangelicals have attached their
religion.

One night, a television personality spoke tenaciously against religion when, ironically, he is religious in his own way of putting down
religions. Among those who have not had a spiritual experience and
allowed it to enlighten them, God and religion are often and mis-
takenly meshed into one. Bigoted and heretical things that religious

people do in the name of the Lord are sometimes the same actions and words of the nonreligious or antireligious and, therefore, only affirm that those things are not of the Lord. There is God, and there is religion. There is what is seen as good in God's eyes, and there is what the religious believe to be good in God's eyes. Religion is like the letter of the law; it kills.

I know this to be true, as I see it and have experienced its prominence within the Christian community; however, I do not believe all Christians to be guilty of these things. Racism, classism, sexism, and misogyny are recurring themes of our country's history. To consider these to also be themes of the modern Christian church seems a bit unfair. I know that Christ did not approve of the ways in which people twist the words of scripture to exempt themselves; however, there is hypocrisy with the people and what they consider "religion."

There is nothing wrong with being a Christ follower; it just depends on what we believe to be Christ-like. Men are on the way to completely destroying faith, especially the three major faiths of the world—the Abrahamic religions of Judaism, Christianity, and Islam. God is not a god of "do's" and "don'ts." We must be people of "wills" and "won'ts." That is only after our experience with Him.

Very few people are comfortable with themselves. They long for something to make themselves feel good, and church is a place where people may go to get that. Evangelicals, however, use religion in a toxic way. Many people need something to boast their self-worth. I know this because I used to be one of them. I am not always comfortable with every aspect of myself, but I've learned to be content with it.

Some people are so poor that all they have is money. For these toxic evangelicals, I will change this statement to, "Some people are woeful; all they have is their self-righteousness." No exaltation of oneself is ever appropriate over other human beings, even when it is fueled by a pride in one's relationship with God. After all, scripture tells us that love is patient, kind, and does not boast.

The danger of bad religion is that people hold onto what they were taught religiously even when those things don't coincide with what they were taught divinely. This world—this society in which we live and participate—demands us to choose sides; sometimes it's a bipartisanship, and sometimes it comes in multiple categories.

As I recall some of our nation's most beloved figures and leaders throughout history, I wonder what they would make of what is happening right now. We are all meant to exist in a time in which we fulfill our purpose. These figures and leaders handled the problems of our yesterday; we are here to resolve the problems of our today. Dr. King was an activist for human rights and civil rights, and I don't know how he would've looked at our current situation.

One of the challenges as a pastor is that we have ourselves to contend with as well as others in our churches, communities, and the general public eye. It is easy to be concerned with how people view us rather than in what we believe, which many pastors do. In every message we study, we may be astute in Greek and Hebrew, know how to exegete the scripture, or know how to use the tools to be great orators and deliver powerful excitement, but the message doesn't have powerful change until the preaching moment comes. The preaching moment is when God steps in. It is a spiritual experience shared with all present. When we finish what we're preaching, we don't even know what we said. That's how it is for me.

Some people may be offended by my words and question the extent of my faith in Jesus. As a brother in Christ, my faith in God is unbreakable; however, I stand by what I say. Had I not been raised to be Christian, there would be no appeal for me to become one. If what I had been taught is true, then I'd be on my way to hell. The religion I was raised on seemed to be against me—a man of color and a person who embraced people from every walk of life, which are two major strikes. Then, to have someone judge me was often a lot to handle. Sometimes, all one wants is to be accepted. Jesus came to embrace us on the cross on Calvary. He had already said, "If I am lifted up from the earth, I will draw all people unto me."

People have asked me, "How do you know Jesus is real?"

My response was once something like, "How do you know George Washington is?"

We've never seen these people or Cleopatra, Marc Antony, the prophet Muhammad (peace be upon him), Moses, or Caesar. I know they're real because it is in my heart.

An ossuary was found that contained bones believed to belong to James—Jesus's half-brother—because on the outside it read, "James the brother of Jesus." There was only one way they could say that. When James passed away, they had to believe that Jesus was still alive; that is why he was mentioned. Although he was crucified, he rose from the dead and somebody believed he was still alive before they put that on there. All there is in existence is revelation that God is real.

I have a relationship with God through Christ Jesus. He is The Way, The Truth, and The Life. By faith, I know the things I hold to be true; by grace, I came to have faith in the first place. Despite my upbringing, the doctrines I was taught in the church and the ways I have seen religious folk claiming to do work in the name of the Lord, I would have fallen away from Jesus; however, I didn't. God graced me to see Jesus, be moved, and help move others so that we could all follow Jesus. The churches we build mean nothing to the work that we do for the Lord. The church is just a structure; the real monuments of Christ are his followers.

These are my thoughts, and I am asking for consideration. I hope these words can transcend the minds and hearts in need of a change. Love is best gifted when it is also returned.

Made in the USA
Columbia, SC
14 November 2022

71193911R00033